Squirrel

Susan Gates

Illustrated by
Tony Kerins

OXFORD
UNIVERSITY PRESS

OXFORD
UNIVERSITY PRESS

Great Clarendon Street, Oxford, OX2 6DP,
United Kingdom

Oxford University Press is a department of the University of Oxford.
It furthers the University's objective of excellence in research, scholarship,
and education by publishing worldwide. Oxford is a registered trade mark of
Oxford University Press in the UK and in certain other countries

Text © Susan Gates 2003

The moral rights of the author have been asserted

First published in this edition 2016

British Library Cataloguing in Publication Data
Data available

978-0-19-837703-0

5 7 9 10 8 6

Paper used in the production of this book is a natural, recyclable product
made from wood grown in sustainable forests. The manufacturing process
conforms to the environmental regulations of the country of origin.

Printed in China by Leo Paper Products Ltd.

Acknowledgements
Cover and inside illustrations by Tony Kerins
Inside cover notes written by Gill Howell

Contents

1 Squirrel Comes to Stay   5

2 Squirrel Becomes a
   Pain in the Neck   11

3 Squirrel Does His Worst
   Thing Yet   16

4 Squirrel Gets a Second
   Chance   20

5 Squirrel Is Back Where
   He Belongs   26

About the author   32

Chapter 1

Squirrel Comes to Stay

Dad undid his coat.

"Alex! Look what I've got," he said.
There was a squirrel hanging on to Dad's
jumper! The squirrel was tiny, just a baby.
He was fast asleep.

"Awww," I said. "He's really cute.
Where did you get him, Dad?"

"It's a sad story," said Dad. "Listen …"

Dad was walking in the forest. He met some men cutting down trees. One of the men said, "Want a squirrel?"

"Excuse me?" said Dad.

"A baby squirrel," said the man. "The tree we cut down had a squirrel's nest in it. His mother was killed. He's too little to look after himself."

"Give him to me," said Dad. "I'll look after him."

So that's how Dad came home with Squirrel.

Dad was at work all day. Mum was busy. So I had to look after Squirrel.

At first it wasn't hard. He slept all day, like a newborn baby. He even went to sleep in my pocket!

"Hey," I told Dad. "Squirrel thinks I'm a tree, and my pocket is his nest."

I went outside with Squirrel in
my pocket. I walked up and down
the street.

"Alex!" said my friend. "There's a tail
hanging out of your pocket!"

"It's only Squirrel," I said. "He thinks
I'm a tree."

Sometimes, Squirrel would wake up and eat a nut. Then he'd go to sleep again. At night, he slept in our old hamster cage.

I told Dad, "Looking after baby squirrels is easy. They're no trouble at all."

Chapter 2

Squirrel Becomes a Pain in the Neck

Then Squirrel got bigger. He didn't sleep so much, and he wouldn't stay in my pocket.

"Mum!" I shouted. "Come quick!"

Squirrel had run down my leg! Then he'd run back up – INSIDE my trousers!

"Help!" I shouted. "He's run up my trousers!"

I could feel his sharp little claws.

"He's under my T-shirt now!"

Then, POP! Squirrel came out by my neck. He sat on my shoulder. Then he climbed a bit higher.

"He's on top of my head!"

"I can see that," said Mum. "He thinks you're a tree."

Squirrel got even braver. He stopped climbing on me, and he started to climb the curtains.

"Mum!" I shouted. "Look at Squirrel!"

Mum came rushing in.

Squirrel was sitting on the curtain rail.
He was eating a nut. There were bits of
nut all over the carpet.

Mum said, "Look at the mess your
squirrel's making!"

"*My* squirrel!" I said. "Dad brought
him home!"

I tried to stop Squirrel. I really did. But I couldn't. He was wrecking our house. No one thought he was cute any more.

"Squirrel will have to go," said Dad.

"Oh, but Dad," I begged. "He's too little to look after himself."

Chapter 3

Squirrel Does His Worst Thing Yet

Then, Squirrel did something really dangerous.

Mum's friend came to visit with her new baby.

Mum said, "Shut Squirrel up in his cage."

I meant to do it. I really did. But there was something good on TV. So I forgot.

Mum's friend came into the room. She was carrying her new baby. He had a pink, bald head.

Suddenly, Squirrel jumped from the curtains. He flew through the air, with his claws out. He was looking for somewhere to land.

"Watch out!" cried Mum. "Mind the baby's head!"

Just in time, the baby's mum turned around. Squirrel missed the baby's head. But he landed on the baby's mum's back.

"Get it off me!" she shouted.

I said, "He can't help it. He thinks you're a tree."

But no one was listening.

"I'm sorry, Alex," said Dad, after they'd gone. "That baby could have been badly hurt. Squirrel will have to go!"

Chapter 4

Squirrel Gets a Second Chance

So we took Squirrel back to the forest. We left him under a tree with a pile of nuts. He looked so small and sad, sitting there.

I told Dad, "He doesn't know about forests. He's never even climbed a tree!"

"He'll be all right," said Dad. "Walk away and don't look back."

All night, I worried about Squirrel. It
was stormy outside. I thought, "What if
he's scared?"

Next morning, I begged Dad, "Can we go to the forest? Please! Just to see if he's all right? Please?"

Dad said, "All right. But you'll never find him. He's probably miles away by now."

But Squirrel was still there! He was just where we'd left him.

"See, Dad!" I said. "I told you he was too little to look after himself."

There were some ladies sitting at a picnic table. I walked past them.

"Squirrel!" I said.

He was really pleased to see me.
He ran straight up my trousers!

The ladies' mouths hung open.

Their eyes almost popped out
of their heads.

"Did you see what that squirrel
just did?"

I tried to look cool. I tried to look as if squirrels ran up my trouser legs all the time.

"He thinks I'm a tree," I told them. I walked off, with Squirrel sitting on my head.

Chapter 5

Squirrel Is Back Where He Belongs

Two weeks later, Mum said, "I'm sick of finding nuts down the sofa."

Dad said, "He's chewed up my computer leads again."

I knew we couldn't put it off any longer. This time, Squirrel really had to go.

We took him to the forest again.
We put him under a tree. I said to Dad,
"He won't climb it!"

But then, with a flick of his tail,
he was gone.

"He's there. No, there!" I said.

He shot right to the top of the tree.
Then he was leaping from treetop to
treetop. It was as if he'd lived in the
forest all his life.

Suddenly, I couldn't see him any more.
"He's gone," I said, sadly.

We walked back to the car. Dad said, "He belongs in the forest. You can't keep squirrels as pets."

I said, "I know that."

But that doesn't stop me thinking about Squirrel. I often wonder where he is. And I hope he's safe and well.

If you're ever walking in a forest and a squirrel runs up your trousers, you'll tell me, won't you?

About the author

This story is true. Everything in it really happened. When my son Alex was six his dad did bring back a baby squirrel. It started off by being cute and ended up wrecking our house. Take my advice. Never, ever, try to keep a squirrel as a pet. Unless you want chewed chair legs and peanuts in your piano!